D0910657

1800-1850 Americans Move Westward

Written by NAUNERLE FARR

Edited by D'ANN CALHOUN

Illustrated by FRANK REDONDO

Editorial consultant LAWRENCE W. BLOCH

A VINCENT FAGO PRODUCTION

Pendulum Press, Inc.
West Haven, Connecticut

COPYRIGHT ©1976 BY PENDULUM PRESS, INC.
All rights reserved. No part of this
book may be reproduced in any
form whatsoever without written
permission from the publisher.

ISBN 0-88301-227-8

Published by
PENDULUM PRESS, INC.
An Academic Industries, Inc., Company
The Academic Building
Saw Mill Road
West Haven, Connecticut 06516

Printed in the United States of America

To the Teacher:

With educators everywhere concerned about the literacy of the nation's children, attention has been focused primarily on the reading curriculum. Reading teachers can select from literally thousands of varied programs for their classes. Yet social studies teachers, faced with an equal amount of material to cover, are often at a loss. Although many history texts are available, they all seem to offer information alone at the expense of motivation. Out of this understanding the **Basic Illustrated History of America** series was developed.

Motivation is the basic premise and the outstanding strength of these texts. Each book was written in the belief that children will learn and remember whatever they find enjoyable. Through illustration, they are drawn into the reading matter, and learning begins.

Besides motivating, the illustrations provide clues to the meanings of words. Unfamiliar vocabulary is defined in footnotes. Every volume in the series has been edited to simplify the reading. And, since the interest level extends as far as the adult reader, students in all grades—even in remedial classes—will enjoy these texts. Finally, companion student activity books guide the reading with vocabulary drills and exercises on comprehension.

The **Basic Illustrated History of America** series, then, offers a new concept in the teaching of American history, yet one which does not subordinate content to form. Meticulously researched historical data provides the authenticity for costumes and architecture in each era. Together, the features of this unique series will make learning an enjoyable experience for the student—and a rewarding one for the teacher.

The editors

contents

America buys the Louisiana territory from France in 1803; Lewis and Clark set out to explore the new lands 6-25

Roads and canals spread across the country; by 1850 railroads join the major eastern cities 26-31

Friendly Indians show the white men how to hunt for buffalo; fur traders work hard in the wilderness 32-46

Missionaries travel westward to bring Christianity to the waiting Indians. 47-52

Other settlers looking for a new life soon follow the missionaries to the West 53-57

The Oregon territory becomes American land, and the United States finally stretches from sea to sea 58-59

Questions for study. 60-61

Thomas Jefferson, president of the United States in 1802, received important news.
We are sure of it, Mr. President. The story is true.
France has taken over New Orleans and the Louisiana Territory from Spain!
And all our western settlers must send their goods through New Orleans.
Whoever owns that port is our enemy!
We can hardly fight France if she decides to close it!

In Paris a few weeks later, Robert Livingston, minister to France, received a letter.

* famous French foreign minister

A special messenger brought an order to James Monroe.

** a special ambassador

Tallyrand usually spoke softly, and Livingston was a little deaf. Had he heard correctly?

This was the news that greeted Monroe when he arrived in Paris two days later.

We were not told to buy so much—or to spend so much.

But we would more than double our size! We would remove the rule of all other countries from the Mississippi valley! It is the chance of a lifetime!

Talks took place with Tallyrand. They agreed on a price of fifteen million dollars—about four cents an acre. This was the biggest real estate deal in history!

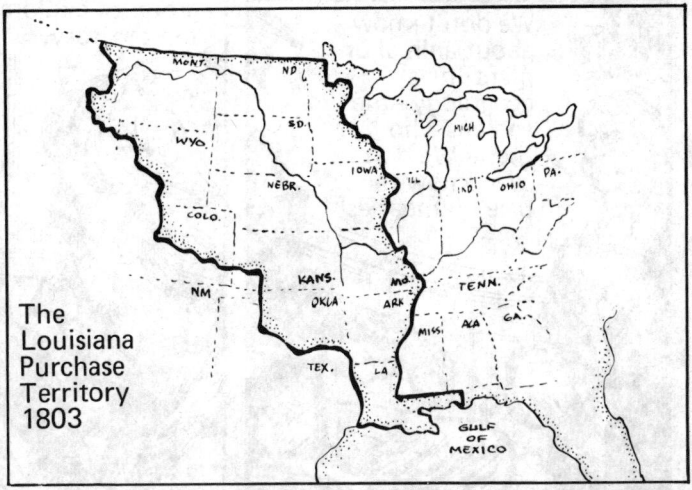

The Louisiana Purchase Territory 1803

Thomas Jefferson was very curious about the western lands. He had always wanted to know more about them. Now they were part of the United States, and they were still unknown to most Americans.

You are my choice to head the group, Meriwether.
I would be glad to do so, sir. Could I have William Clark as a partner?

He is a younger brother of George Rogers Clark, and he knows frontier life very well!
He is a good choice. Pick your own men.

At Jefferson's request, Congress voted $2,500 for the expenses of the group. Lewis made the preparations. They set up headquarters at St. Louis. In the spring of 1804, they were ready to move up the Missouri River on the first stage of their trip across the unknown lands. They had a keelboat, two lighter boats and tons of supplies.
The Missouri had a swift current, sandbars, snags, whirlpools, collapsing banks. Sometimes they went thirty miles in a day; often, only five or six.

Besides twenty-eight soldiers and several boatmen, there was Clark's black servant, York, and Lewis's dog, Scammon.

The river provided all sorts of fish, including the biggest catfish they had ever seen.

They made notes of everything, this being one of the purposes of the trip. They were surprised at the many birds they saw.

These rare birds were once common in the midwestern states.

Another important job was to note the different kinds of Indians they met. They were to make friends with them if they could, for these Indians were now part of the United States.

On June 12 they met a raft headed south, loaded with furs and Frenchmen.

'Allo, Americains! Bonjour, M'sieus*!

Hello, the raft! Greetings, Frenchmen!

The two boats tied up for a visit. The captains wanted to learn everything possible about the trip ahead.

What about the Indians upriver?

High up you'll find the Mandans. They are good Indians. But before the Mandans you'll be in Sioux country!

And the Sioux?

The Sioux are sly and mean. They will ask for gifts.

And there are thousands of them! You won't get through Sioux country without trouble.

* Hello, Americans! Good day, sirs!

* conference with Indians

We bring you American flags and medals. The American father wants his children to live in peace together . . .
They gave gifts to the Indians.
Then one of the chiefs stepped forward.
You insult us with cheap gifts! You must give much more—tobacco and whiskey! But no matter how much, you will not be allowed to go upriver!
The Sioux have many warriors—as many as the leaves on the trees!
If white men go upriver, you will be followed and killed! All, all of you!

The moment was tense. Clark drew his sword; the guards raised their rifles.

We're Americans! This is our nation! We'll share it with you in peace and friendship. But if you try to fight us, we'll wipe you off the earth!

Lewis and Clark returned safely to their boat. There they talked.

First the Sioux chiefs said they would fight. Then they begged for peace. They came aboard, left again, and tried to keep the boats from moving. The group was always on guard. When the boats moved, the Indians followed along the banks for four days. But at last they went away.

At times the temperature was fifty degrees below zero. When the weather was good, they worked on canoes.

On March 3 there was a welcome sight.

Charbonneau, a French trapper, was in the Mandan village. He talked to Lewis.

She was captured when she was a child. But she remembers the Shoshone language and some of the country. If she went with you, this might be helpful.

So it was that Sacajawea joined the group, with her two-month-old baby.
I will be happy to go back to the land of my fathers with you!

In April they started upriver again. Time after time they had to get out and push.
This is ice water!
The rocky bottom cuts my feet to pieces!

After months of travel they reached Montana and the Shoshone Indians.
We must make them know we are friendly.
Where is Sacajawea?

Suddenly she rushed forward.
Do you not know me, my brother? I am your little sister, come home after all these winters!

I know you well. Welcome home, little sister.
My brother, the white men speak with straight tongues. You should be their friend.
Tell them that the Indians welcome their white brothers to this country.
The group needed horses for crossing the Rocky Mountains. The Shoshones had horses—but only a few.
My brother, the white men must have horses!
We will let them have what they need.
Now came the hardest part of the trip.
Don't . . . know if I can make it!
Do you think it will get much colder?

Tired, hungry, ill, they could not yet know what they had done. They had crossed the Rockies. They were near the headwaters of the Columbia River, on the last part of their journey. The Indians took them in, fed and cared for them.

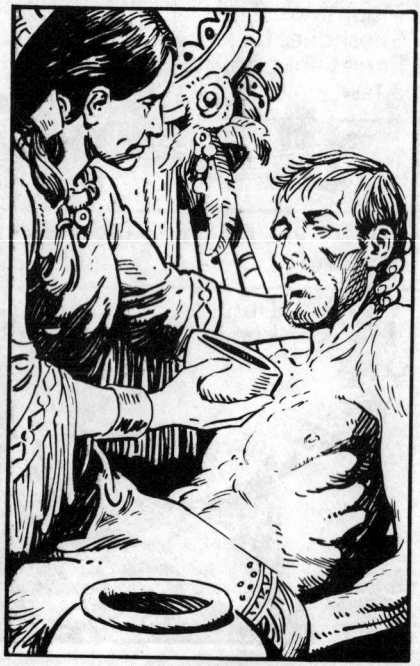

* a tribe of Indians who lived in the northwest

Soon they were strong enough to build new canoes. They were ready to sail the swiftly-flowing streams and rivers that would carry them, they hoped, to the Pacific Ocean.

They built another fort and settled in. They named it Fort Clatsop for the nearby Indians.

If a ship arrives, at least some of us can return by sea.

The Indians have been asked to let us know if one stops anywhere along this coast.

FORT CLATS

They spent long hours boiling salt out of sea water.

We'll keep hunters out every day. Then we can preserve the extra meat with sea salt.

The cold, rainy winter passed.

It is March again, but no ships!

It's time to start back the way we came!

So they packed up and started back, up the swift rivers and over the mountains. This time they made a quicker and easier trip. At last they reached the Missouri again, and the Mandan village. Here they parted from Charbonneau, Sacajawea, and the baby Baptiste, now old enough to do a baby war dance.

On September 23, 1806, they reached St. Louis at the mouth of the Missouri River.

Thomas Jefferson, and the country, would say much more about it.

* refuse to let a bill become a law

** according to the United States Constitution

The National or Cumberland Road, today U.S. 40, was a success. Horses and wagons could travel at ten miles an hour. It was much better than any other road we had, and added greatly to the flow of western travel.

On August 9, 1807, people along the Hudson River in New York watched a great event.

* a waterway built for travel

It took eight years to finish the Erie Canal. On October 26, 1826, a large number of canal boats started from Buffalo.

In every village the mules were frightened by cheering crowds.

The canal was a great success. At once the cost of sending goods dropped $100 a ton to $8. It made New York a great city, and carried thousands of passengers west.

In 1828, the Baltimore and Ohio Railroad Company started building tracks. It was slow work.

In 1830, the Baltimore and Ohio put its first small locomotive* into service. It was called *Tom Thumb.*

By 1850 there would be 9,000 miles of track connecting the major cities of the East. It would carry goods and people between East and West.

* train engine

St. Louis, on the frontier*, was the "gateway to the West." Lewis and Clark started and ended their trip there. In 1819, William Ashley of Missouri went into a St. Louis newspaper office.

It would become the Ashley Rocky Mountain Company. And among the men Ashley talked to were names that would change the future of the West. One of them was Jim Beckwourth.

* a border land between wild and lived-in places

Jed Smith, Jim Bridger, Bill Sublette, Tom Fitzpatrick—these were other men who would try it. Some worked for companies, some alone. In their love of the forests and their search for valuable furs, they would explore the far west to the Pacific. They would find the passes through the mountains and open the way for the settlers who would follow. They were the mountain men.

By mid-September they reached their first stop, the Pawnee camp at Ottumwa.

Ashley's party received friendly greetings as the Indians stared at the black man.
A buffalo hunt?
Yes, to bring in their winter meat supply.
Where is Chief Two-Axe?
In lodge. Will you come?
You come with us, Jim.
They were soon seated inside the Chief's lodge.
Welcome to our camp, General. You come early this year.
We wanted to hire some guides from you. We're going northwest into Montana country.

*dried meat mixed with spices and berries

Like an army, the mounted braves, yelping dogs and squaws** moved across the grassy plain.

* a type of stretcher made of hides attached to poles

** Indian women

For two hours the crowd moved north. Then two scouts appeared.

Is there danger of driving them over the cliffs?

No, we will kill all we need before the buffalo reach the cliffs.

Take your braves and circle the herd from the hills.

Bands of hunters, now on their fastest ponies, moved quietly toward the nearby hills.

From Tekhia Ridge, Jim saw his first large buffalo herd. They covered the plain like a gray blanket, still in the noonday heat. All was quiet; no Indians were in sight.
Chief Two-Axe looked around him. He held up a spear.
He threw the spear high into the sky. There was a great cry.
AIEEEee-ee-ee!

Even before the spear curved downward, the hills exploded with Indians. The braves rode toward the buffalo from three sides, with screeching cries and galloping hoofs. The buffalo ran off. The hunt had begun!

Holding his spear with one hand and his pony's mane with the other, each brave rode into the herd of buffalo.
Choosing one animal each, the hunters drove their spears into the necks of the buffalo.
AII-EE-eeeeeeeeeeee!

Finally Two-Axe gave new orders.

Now the squaws will load the meat and take it to the drying frames.
You see how they hang it up there.
They'll keep the fires going all night, smoking and drying the meat.
Guests and workers alike feasted on buffalo.
Best meat I ever tasted!
There's nothing like fresh buffalo meat!

The next morning the squaws pounded the dried meat into powder and mixed it with spices and berries. Then they coated it with melted buffalo fat, and packed it into buffalo skin cases.

Suddenly from behind there was a scuffling sound.
She slipped! She was carrying our food!

Quickly the mule was swept away.
All our food was on that mule!

We're at least a week from Fort Clark.
We can't make it without food. We must hunt.

They camped that night without food. In the morning, snow was in the air.
All right, men, let's go.
To find game, you must go beyond forest.

* an animal like a deer

Pushing forward carefully, he came out onto a high grassland.
They're so fast! Could I possibly get two?
He took out two bullets. He fired, reloaded, fired again.
Crack!
I did it!
Night came and passed. At camp, the other men worried.
I hope Jim's not lost—or too weak from hunger to get back here.
We'd better look for him. He doesn't know this country.
Weak from cold and hunger, the men followed Jim's trail. Finally they smelled smoke.
Jim! Why didn't you come back? We were worried.
No use making two trips. I knew you'd find me!

Well supplied with meat, Lajeunesse was able to make the trip back to Fort Clark for more food. Meanwhile, the others went on to the winter camp.

In spite of the snow and cold, the winter passed quickly. Every day there was work to do.

The traps must be set and the catch removed . . .

The trapped beavers were skinned and the skins dressed.

But a roaring fire kept the cabin warm.

But Tom Fitzpatrick himself, a few years later, led the first women and the first wagon over the Rockies. He led them into Oregon through the south pass discovered by other Ashley men.

They went by steamboat to Cincinnati, to St. Louis, to Liberty, Missouri, the end of the line. With them went the two Indian boys, and two other missionaries,* Eliza and Henry Spalding.

* people who brought the Christian faith to the Indians

There was only one thing to do. Whitman bought riding horses and a wagon for luggage. Then they started off across the plains.
There were dangerous rivers to cross.
Don't worry, Marcus! We'll make it!
After days of hard riding, they met the first challenge and caught up with the fur trappers. Its leader was Tom Fitzpatrick.
You've given us the honor, ma'am, of being the first group ever to take white women over the mountains!
Through the heat and dust the trappers followed the River Platte.
They say the Platte is a thousand miles long and six inches deep!

On the treeless plain, Narcissa and Eliza learned to make fires out of dried buffalo droppings.
Fresh buffalo meat every day! What a luxury!
I don't think it agrees with me.

After two months they were riding through the south pass, the gateway to Oregon. Just ahead was the fur trappers' meeting place.
What happens at the meeting place, Tom?
Why, ma'am, the trappers get together and enjoy themselves after a hard winter.

They'll sell their furs . . . eat and drink and play cards. Some of them will spend in a few days the money they've worked all winter to make!
More important to the Whitmans, the meeting place was the end of the trail for the fur trappers.
I've met two English fur traders from the Hudson's Bay Company. Perhaps they'll let us go on to Oregon with them.

They set out with the English party. Six weeks' travel over the roughest part of the trail lay ahead.

The last part of the journey was down the Columbia River.

At Fort Vancouver, they were greeted by the British agent, Dr. McLoughlin.

* a program of lessons in religion and school work

Whitman was delighted by the rich soil.

The Whitmans and others sent word back East of the wonders of Oregon. In September, 1842, a band of settlers just over the mountains arrived.

But Marcus had decided. He would save the mission—and he would do more! He would go to Washington and see the president. There he would show Congress that this was the time to claim Oregon for the United States!

In May, 1843, a great wagon train gathered at Independence, Missouri. It was ready to roll west with 2,000 animals, 1,000 people, and 100 wagons. They kept turning to one man for advice—Marcus Whitman.

They passed the great plains sights.

Scott's Bluff . . .

Chimney Rock . . .

Independence Rock, where the men carved their names.

The Snake River was the worst river yet. It was fast, wide, and deep. They chained the wagons together.

But they made it. A thousand settlers, 100 wagons, had come over the Oregon trail safely. Many more would follow.

In the Columbia River at Oregon City, two warships waited: the British *Modeste,* and the American *Shark.*

In Oregon City, the people went wild with excitement. The American flag was raised. Cannons fired from the *Shark*.

It's settled! We're Americans! Right through to the Pacific Ocean!

* an imaginary line around the earth which measures distance from the equator

Words to know

1. antelope
2. canal
3. constitutional
4. frontier
5. locomotive
6. mission
7. missionaries
8. Nez Perce
9. parallel
10. pemmican
11. squaw
12. veto

Questions

1. Why did President Jefferson want to buy New Orleans from the French?
2. What made France offer to sell the whole Louisiana Territory to the U.S.?
3. Why were Lewis and Clark sent to explore the Louisiana Territory?
4. Name some of the Indian tribes who lived in the central and western parts of the country. Were they friendly or unfriendly?
5. How did the Indian woman Sacajawea help Lewis and Clark?
6. What were some of the inventions and discoveries that made trade and travel easier during the early 1800s?
7. Why were the missionaries of this time so eager to travel into the West?
8. What were some of the methods of travel used to reach the West?
9. What territory won from England first extended the United States from the Atlantic to the Pacific?
10. What animal did the plains Indians make great use of for food, shelter, and clothing?

Match the following people and objects with the things they are famous for:

1. *Clermont*
2. railroad locomotive
3. Mr. McAdam
4. De Witt Clinton
5. Columbia
6. Livingston and Monroe
7. Robert Fulton
8. *Tom Thumb*
9. Talleyrand
10. Lewis and Clark

a. name of first locomotive
b. name of first steamboat
c. invented the steamboat
d. sold Louisiana Territory to the U.S.
e. explored the Louisiana Territory
f. arranged to build the Erie Canal
g. nicknamed the "iron horse"
h. bought Louisiana Territory from France
i. invented a new type of road
j. river which flows into the Pacific Ocean

Complete the following sentences

1. Besides the explorers and missionaries, _____ helped to open up trails to the West for settlers.
2. The city known as the "gateway to the West" is _____.
3. Two crops which grew very well in the midwest and in the northwest were _____ and _____.
4. The Erie Canal connected Lake Erie with _____.
5. The Americans learned a great deal about their new country from the _____.